1850~1876
The Civil War

Written by NAUNERLE FARR

Edited by D'ANN CALHOUN

Illustrated by NESTOR REDONDO

Editorial consultant LAWRENCE W. BLOCH

A VINCENT FAGO PRODUCTION

Pendulum Press, Inc.

West Haven, Connecticut

ISBN 0-88301-228-6

Published by
PENDULUM PRESS, INC.
An Academic Industries, Inc., Company
The Academic Building
Saw Mill Road
West Haven, Connecticut 06516

Printed in the United States of America

To the Teacher:

With educators everywhere concerned about the literacy of the nation's children, attention has been focused primarily on the reading curriculum. Reading teachers can select from literally thousands of varied programs for their classes. Yet social studies teachers, faced with an equal amount of material to cover, are often at a loss. Although many history texts are available, they all seem to offer information alone at the expense of motivation. Out of this understanding the **Basic Illustrated History of America** series was developed.

Motivation is the basic premise and the outstanding strength of these texts. Each book was written in the belief that children will learn and remember whatever they find enjoyable. Through illustration, they are drawn into the reading matter, and learning begins.

Besides motivating, the illustrations provide clues to the meanings of words. Unfamiliar vocabulary is defined in footnotes. Every volume in the series has been edited to simplify the reading. And, since the interest level extends as far as the adult reader, students in all grades—even in remedial classes—will enjoy these texts. Finally, companion student activity books guide the reading with vocabulary drills and exercises on comprehension.

The **Basic Illustrated History of America** series, then, offers a new concept in the teaching of American history, yet one which does not subordinate content to form. Meticulously researched historical data provides the authenticity for costumes and architecture in each era. Together, the features of this unique series will make learning an enjoyable experience for the student—and a rewarding one for the teacher.

The editors

contents

On a cold January night in the 1850s, people crowded into Boston's Faneuil Hall. They were coming to hear a talk by the famous orator,* Wendell Phillips.

Ralph Waldo Emerson, the well-known writer, was the chairman.**

And now may I present . . . Mr. Wendell Phillips.

My friends, may I tell you about a recent happening? In Kentucky the owner of a large plantation has died. His 500 slaves are to be sold. Try to imagine how the white men will sell them . . .

* a person who makes many speeches
** the person in charge of a program

A man with a black whip shows the unhappy negroes as if they were animals . . .

He shows that their teeth are good, and tells their ages and weight . . .

An interested buyer might check his back for lash marks. Signs of too many beatings would show that the slave was a troublemaker.

Each slave goes to the highest bidder. Families are broken up, in spite of their tears and begging.

Sold "down the river", the slaves are chained and marched away.

And what is the life that waits for these poor Africans on the cotton plantations down the river?

Picture the owner's beautiful house—and the row of small cabins behind. The slaves are given food—perhaps a quart of corn meal and half a pound of salt pork a day. They wear the cheapest clothing. They get shoes for the winter months only.

For this the slave works from dawn to dusk. He does his master's bidding his whole life long, unless he is sold once again.

Mr. Phillips finished his talk. There was much clapping.

The meeting was opened for questions. A cotton mill owner stood up.

This cannot be true! The Southerners are not monsters! I have visited many plantations and the slaves are well-housed and well-fed. They have their own gardens!

They have doctors when they are sick. When they are too old to work, they are cared for. They lead a healthy, outdoor life!

I have visited plantations with my husband, and he is right! The slaves are like happy children!

And yet, madam, these "happy children" run away. They've even been known to fight their owners.

It is not a matter of how well or how badly the slaves are treated. They are human beings like us!

Slaves are God's people, too! No man has the right to own another man!

The more some people argued against slavery, the more others argued for it.

There is slavery in the Bible! Cain* had to suffer, and so must they!

* a man who was forced to suffer because he killed his brother Abel

For a long time the sons of wealthy southern planters had gone to college in the North. Some came home with upsetting ideas.

If your teacher talked against slavery, John, don't let me hear any of it! Our people are happy!

But father, if the slaves are so happy, why do they run away?

Oh, John!

Those are only a few trouble-makers!

Even John would not talk about the secret fear of many southerners, the slave revolts. As many as 200 revolts took place during the years that slavery was practiced. Few won freedom for any slaves. But they showed that not all blacks accepted their lot without protest. One of the largest, in Virginia in 1831, was led by Nat Turner.

Turner learned to read and write even though laws kept slaves from doing so. Studying the Bible, he came to believe that God was telling him what to do.

From a great black cloud an angel leaned out, and told me what God wants!

Lord, lord!

Over a period of time, he made his plans.

Each place we go along this road, we pick up horses and guns.

There are 10,000 blacks in this county. Once we start, thousands will join us! Before the whites know it, we'll reach town and take the arsenal!*

The night arrived.

Let the angel of the Lord chase them . . . Now. Let us begin the battle!

What you all think you're doin' in here!

* a place where guns and gunpowder are stored

From house to house they went, leaving dead behind them, fifty-seven in all!

Daylight came, but not the revolt that Turner had expected.

Where is that crowd supposed to join us? Ain't more than seventy-five of us at most!

Wait! They'll come!

But they did not come. Finally the soldiers captured Turner and his men. Many blacks had fought to protect their masters instead of joining the revolt.

That's the spirit! Fire away, lads!

Look at dem blacks shootin' at us!

In 1838, a slave named Frederick Bailey ran away. Dressed as a sailor, he went by train to Massachusetts.

May I ask your name, sir?

It's Frederick ... uh ... Frederick Douglass!

And I suppose you are going to the port of New Bedford. Well, God keep you, Frederick Douglass!

Thank you, sir!

The new name was part of his disguise.* It was to become famous.

Douglass got a job in a shipyard. He had already taught himself to read. Now he read whenever he could.

"The Liberator." Is that a good paper?

It's a fine paper —if you believe slaves ought to be free!

It's put out by William Lloyd Garrison. Take it and read it.

Thank you, I will!

* something which changes the way a person looks

Reading *The Liberator,* he became a great admirer of Garrison. He also began to speak against slavery himself, in church meeting halls.

A good speech, Mr. Douglass!

Thank you.

Here is someone who wants to meet you. Mr. Douglass, William Lloyd Garrison.

Mr. Garrison! I have wanted to meet you for a long time!

You have a fine voice, sir. You speak well. I would like you to join me on a tour.

Douglass and Garrison became friends and worked against slavery. They spoke to people in the North and West.

Later, Douglass had his own newspaper. He wrote about freedom for the slaves.

We're ready to print. What have you decided about a name?

My paper will be called *The North Star* because it points the way to freedom.

In Washington, many things were happening. Visitors to the United States senate in the winter of 1850 pointed out three people—the Old Giants.

There he is—Daniel Webster, the senator from Massachusetts. America's greatest orator!

Yes... "Liberty and Union—now and forever!" He puts saving the Union above all.

Not all of his people feel so. Some would end slavery even if it means breaking the Union!

And over there—see? Senator Calhoun from South Carolina!

Poor thing! They say he is dying, but he won't give up. I like his courage, but not his ideas.

Yes... he'll fight to the very end. He believes that the southern states should decide things for themselves.

And that they have the right to leave the Union if that is the only way!

Look—Kentucky's Henry Clay! He is seventy-three years old and very weak. But he is a great help in talks between the North and the South.

If he can work out an agreement this time, he will indeed be called the "Great Com-promiser*!"

What a problem it is! The western lands want to become states. But the South won't let them be free states, and the North won't let them be slave states!

The Compromise of 1850 was finally worked out. By it, California entered the Union as a free state. The people of the Utah and New Mexico territories could settle the question for themselves. A new Fugitive Slave Law would make it easier for slave owners to get back their runaway slaves.

The North will hate the slave law. But without it, the South would never have agreed!

Daniel, I think we have saved the Union! We have ended the problem of slavery!

Among the people who hated the new slave law was Abe Lincoln in Illinois.

I hate to see these poor people hunted down and caught, but I bite my tongue and keep quiet.

Someday he would do more.

* someone who works out an agreement in which the two sides each give up a little

As it turned out, the Compromise did not settle anything. It only helped to make the problem worse.

In 1854, in the little settlement of Ripon, Wisconsin, Major Alvan Bovay called a meeting.

The Democrats and the Whigs, the two political parties, both have northern and southern members.

The leaders are against slavery, but they are afraid to take a stand. They are afraid of splitting the parties, afraid of splitting the country!

Other meetings were held in many parts of the North.

I see only one way to end slavery—form a new party! We will unite all those who want to fight it!

Let us form a new party to keep slavery out of the territories! We will call ourselves Republicans!

No slavery in the territories! Join the Republican party!

In 1854, these groups got together in a convention, and the Republican party was born.

John Brown was a New England Puritan. He believed God told him to free the slaves. Raising money from wealthy friends, he bought a farm near Harpers Ferry, Virginia.

Only to his sons did he tell the details of his plan.

We will set up a fort in Virginia. Then we will free the nearby slaves and give them guns. With those who join us, we will make raids into the South until all are free!

But, Pa— there are so few of us. Will the slaves leave?

Certainly, God has decided it!

On the night of October 19, 1859, a wagon crossed the bridge of Harpers Ferry.

Brown and his eighteen men quickly captured the guards at the arsenal.

Open up the arsenal, or I'll shoot you!

Brown sent groups into the countryside to free the slaves and capture the owners.

We are here to set you free!

No, sir, please— not me!

Soon there were fifty men in the arsenal. In the morning the local militia attacked the building.

Steady, men. Fight bravely!

A group of marines arrived. They were commanded by Colonel Robert E. Lee. When Brown refused to give up, they knocked down the door.

John Brown was captured. He was tried for treason* and hanged. In the North, people like Abraham Lincoln hated the fighting at Harpers Ferry. But some northerners made John Brown into a saint. In the South, after the raid, people were ready to fight for slavery.

On the day that Brown was hanged, services were held in many northern churches.

In the South, it was final proof that they could not remain in the Union.

There—you see? That's what the North wants to do to us!

I believe that new Republican party was behind the whole thing!

* fighting against one's own country

Before the election of 1860, Governor Gist of South Carolina wrote to the other southern governors.

If the Republican man, Lincoln, is elected, South Carolina will leave the United States. I am asking the other cotton states what they will do.

In November, Abraham Lincoln was elected president. Quickly, South Carolina called a state convention.

We declare that the bond between South Carolina and other states under the name of "The United States of America" is now ended.

As the news spread, the people of Charleston rushed into the streets to celebrate.

But at sunrise next morning, at Fort Moultrie across the harbor, the United States flag was raised as usual.

By February, 1861, seven states had seceded* from the United States to form the Confederate States of America. In Montgomery, Alabama, Jefferson Davis had become president of the new nation.

The South must make all who are against us smell southern powder and feel southern steel!

The wonderful South! In only a month, we already have a government.

And we've taken millions of dollars worth of United States property with no one to stop us!

Although Abraham Lincoln was president-elect** of the United States, James Buchanan would still be president until March.

Sir, General Twiggs in Texas has turned over nineteen army posts to the southerners!

I have no power to change that.

* left; no longer belonged to
** a man elected president, but whose term of office has not yet begun

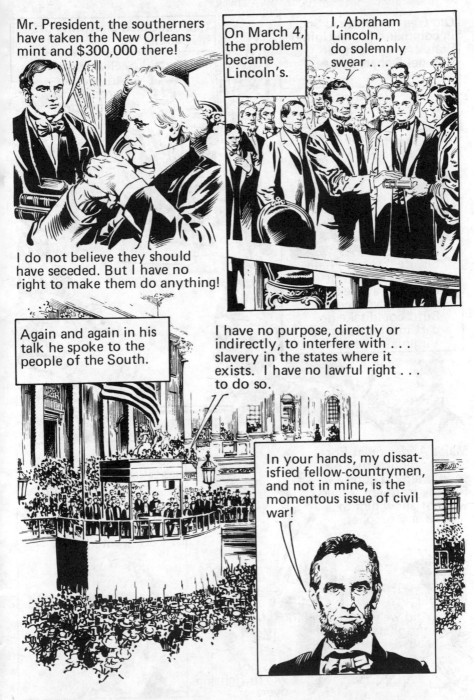

Old General Winfield Scott, in command of the United States Army, sent for Colonel Robert E. Lee.

President Lincoln wishes me to ask you to take command of the army.

Sir, I am sorry. I hate slavery and do not believe that the South should have seceded. But I could take no part in a battle against Virginia—or the South.

Lincoln called a meeting of his cabinet*.

Gentlemen, there is a problem in Charleston harbor!

Major Anderson at Fort Sumter reports that his food is almost gone. But the southern leaders will not allow him to receive any supplies.

Give up the fort!

It is not worth fighting over!

The Confederacy** has taken federal property all over the South and I have not fought back. But I will not see Major Anderson starved out of Fort Sumter!

*the men who help the president with his work ** the name given to the states that left the Union

Lincoln sent a special message to Governor Pickens in Charleston.

An attempt will be made to supply Fort Sumter with food only. No effort will be made to add men, arms, or ammunition . . .

The message was sent on to Montgomery, where president Davis called a cabinet meeting.

Has the time come for an attack on Fort Sumter?

Robert Toombs, Confederate Secretary of State, was opposed.

. . . It will lose us every friend in the North. You will strike a hornet's nest. . . . It is unnecessary. It is in the wrong. It is fatal!

But Davis told General Beauregard something else.

President Davis wants Fort Sumter to surrender. In case they do not, we will attack the fort!

Major Anderson would not give up. On an island in the harbor, Fort Sumter was within easy reach of many southern guns. At dawn on April 12, 1861, the guns opened fire. The fighting had started.

The fort was soon in flames. On the second afternoon, with the walls falling down, Anderson was forced to surrender.

In the North, crowds gathered outside newspaper offices waiting for news.

I can't believe it! They fired on Fort Sumter!

What's the latest news?

Here comes something!

Now we'll have to fight them!

No!

We'll give old Abe everything he needs!

BULLETIN

SUMTER FALLS!

On April 15, Lincoln sent out an announcement.

We want 75,000 state militia to serve in the federal army.

Washington itself, the capital of the Union, was in danger.

We are surrounded by Virginia and Maryland, both slave states. What do we have to defend ourselves with?

On April 19, he announced a blockade on Confederate ports.

Very little, sir—a few companies of soldiers and a handful of marines.

Soldiers are on their way from Massachusetts and New York. But I am afraid of trouble in Baltimore when they cross town to change trains.

On April 19, the Massachusetts Sixth Regiment reached Baltimore. The soldiers started across the city.

A mob, 10,000 strong, attacked the 250 soldiers. They used clubs, stones, and finally bullets.

Hurrah for Jeff Davis!

Get out of our country!

Dig your graves —we'll put you in them!

At last the soldiers loaded their guns and fired.

Four soldiers and ten Southerners were killed. Others were wounded. But the Massachusetts Sixth pushed on to Washington.

But where were the soldiers from New York, from Rhode Island? Lincoln paced the floor.

Why don't they come? Why don't they come?

On April 24, Lincoln visited the wounded men of the Massachusetts Sixth.

I don't believe there is any North! The Seventh Regiment is just a story! You are the only real things!

In Washington, offices and stores were closed. The streets were empty.

It is like a city in wartime!

But two days later the New York Seventh arrived, to be followed by other men. The danger that the capital might be cut off from the North was over. The city came alive again.

Soon there were soldiers living everywhere in Washington. People expected a short war, quickly won.

What are they waiting for? One easy march into Virginia and the Confederacy will fall!

On to Richmond! That's the idea!

By midsummer, the country was still waiting.

Mr. President, we have no army yet. All we have are a few untrained soldiers!

I know—but the North wants an attack!

General Irvin McDowell was in command of the soldiers around Washington.

On July 16, we will attack the Confederate army under General Beauregard, at Manasses.

In two days, the army arrived at a little river known as Bull Run.

The Confederates are dug in on a line beyond the river.

We will attack at early morning!

For a time, things went according to McDowell's plan. The southern line was pushed back.

But a group of Virginians under General T.J. Jackson stood firm.

There is Jackson, standing like a stone wall! Come up behind the Virginians!

"Stonewall" Jackson had a new name. The southern troops fought back. More soldiers arrived.

The day was Sunday. A holiday crowd had driven out from Washington to watch the battle. There were people by the hundreds.

Suddenly there was a change.

Oh, Senator, what a wonderful way to have a picnic!

Yes, indeed! Nice to watch the Johnny Rebs* being defeated!

I say—our soldiers are falling back!

Quick, we must get away!

* a slang name given to the Confederate soldiers

The Union attack had failed. The soldiers fell back. But there was no trouble until they met the holiday crowd returning to Washington. When a broken wagon blocked a bridge, the traffic became tied up. It was every man for himself. The soldiers dropped their guns and ran.

The holiday was over. The North knew for the first time that a long, hard war lay ahead.

In 1861, when Lincoln announced a blockade of the Confederate coast, southerners laughed.

That Lincoln's a fool! The North has about six old wooden tubs ready to sail!

And we've got 3,500 miles of coast, plus the Mississippi with even more miles to cover!

We've got the Norfolk shipyard, too, even if the Union soldiers did burn it when they moved out.

And I hear the Confederate navy men have raised the *Merrimac* that the Yankees* sank, and are fixing her up.

* a slang name for the northern soldiers

The men were right. The southerners had raised the warship *Merrimac* and were hard at work.

We're making her into an ironclad*. We'll name her the *"Virginia,"* and no one will be able to sink her!

Word of the rebuilt *Merrimac* reached Lincoln and naval secretary Gideon Welles.

We're buying and building ships. Our navy is growing fast. But we haven't an ironclad in the lot.

Do you think the *Merrimac* will be successful?

No wooden ship can stand up to her. We'll never win a battle against the *Merrimac.*

Then we must have ironclads! See to it!

John Ericsson, in New York City, was an inventor**. One day he had a visitor.

I'm Cornelius Bushnell. I've come from Washington. Harry Delameter sent me to you.

Yes . . . come in.

* a ship protected with plates of iron
** someone who thinks up new ways of doing things

At Hampton Roads, across the water from the Norfolk navy yard where the *Merrimac* was being made ready, five of the Union's best ships were waiting.

Blockade duty! Most boring thing there is.

I wish there was something exciting to do!

It's coming out! A big ship . . . the *Merrimac!*

The *Merrimac* was an ugly thing. She plowed through the water toward the Union ships. The fire from their guns rattled against her iron sides. Soon one Union ship went down, and another was on fire.

At last, with the tide going out, the *Merrimac* pulled away. But everyone knew she would be back the next day.

The news spread quickly. The next morning, Lincoln and his cabinet waited.

The news is that two of our best ships are sunk, and none of our guns could hurt the *Merrimac*.

We've got to protect Washington! The *Merrimac* could steam up and fire on the White House! I've ordered barges sunk in the Potomac!

Mr. Stanton, this is my job! We're trying to keep the Potomac open! The *Monitor* is on her way to Hampton Roads.

The *Monitor* has two guns, I believe! Two guns, against the *Merrimac's* fifty!

Gentlemen, suppose we wait and see what happens!

The *Monitor* had arrived at Hampton Roads. From the warships, they watched her.

Cheese-box on a raft!

And that's supposed to save us from the *Merrimac*!

The *Merrimac* arrived, ready to attack the Union's *Minnesota*. The *Monitor* headed straight for the *Merrimac*.

The *Merrimac* fired into the *Monitor*. It would have crashed through the *Minnesota*.

The *Monitor's* top turned. Two guns poked out. Two shots were fired into the *Merrimac*.

When the shots were fired, the *Monitor's* guns disappeared, offering no target for the *Merrimac*.

For three hours the battle raged. Then the *Merrimac* left, slowly returning into the harbor, never to fight again. The Navy ordered more *Monitors*. With heavier guns, they could sink anything. It was the end of wooden ships as warships.

General Robert E. Lee commanded the Confederate Army of Virginia. On September 17, 1862, he was defeated at Antietam. Five days later, Lincoln met with his cabinet.

I made a promise to God to free the slaves when the rebels were driven from Maryland. This happened at Antietam.

I am therefore sending out an Emancipation Proclamation saying that upon January 1, 1863, all slaves shall be forever free!

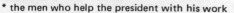

* the men who help the president with his work

** the name given to the states that left the Union

From the beginning of the war, when Union armies invaded the South, runaway slaves had joined them.

At Fortress Monroe, Virginia, Union General Butler was in command when a Confederate officer arrived under a flag of truce.

You have three runaway slaves here, sir. They are valuable property. I ask that they be returned.

By leaving the Union, Virginia became foreign territory. I shall keep the slaves as captured goods.

Camps were later set up for the "captured goods."

After the Emancipation Proclamation, for the first time black soldiers were openly used in the Union army.

Write the governor of Tennessee asking that he send us some negro soldiers. Tell him that the very sight of 50,000 armed black men should end the war at once!

Frederick Douglass had always urged the use of black soldiers. He tried to find more for the Union army.

Why should we join up? They won't let us fight with white soldiers!

They pay us less than the whites!

It's your chance to prove yourselves. And it's your fight! Liberty won by white men would lose half its glory!

Massachusetts raised two groups of black soldiers. Douglass' sons, Charles and Lewis, joined the Massachusetts Thirty-fourth under Colonel Robert Shaw.

Fall in, men. We're off for South Carolina.

At Fort Wagner near Charlestown, the Thirty-fourth led the attack.

I want you to prove yourselves. Move in quick time to within a hundred yards; then double quick, and charge!

When they were two hundred yards from the fort, the Confederates opened fire. Men fell, but the line did not stop.

Sergeant William Carney was the flagbearer. Wounded twice, he still planted the flag at the top of the fort.

For his bravery, Carney won the Congressional Medal of Honor*.

*a special medal for bravery in battle given by the U.S. Congress

On March 3, 1863, the United States passed the first draft law in its history. It was an unfair law and many people did not like it.

Every man between twenty and forty-five has to register.

Put up $300 and you don't have to go.

Or pay somebody to go in your place! You see what that means.

Sure! It's the poor workers who have to fight! And now, to make it worse, we're fighting to free the negroes!

What's wrong with that?

We free 'em, and they'll come up here. They'll work for less money and take our jobs, that's what!

In New York on July 13, while the names were being drawn, a mob drove the marshal from his office.

For days men roamed the streets. They broke into shops and saloons. They burned the homes of anti-slavery leaders and blacks. They killed several hundred people.

The South was winning more battles than the North. But they had problems too, and also a draft law. In June, 1863, deserters* numbered one-third of the army. President Davis announced that no one who returned to the army would be punished. The South was running out of supplies as well.

General Lee decided to attack Pennsylvania.

Our army needs everything—food, shoes, horses. Soldiers can't fight well if they are barefoot and hungry. Pennsylvania is rich.

The farm country provided horses and food. There were even small shoe factories to attack.

On June 27, Lee and his officers studied a map.

Here we shall meet the enemy and fight a great battle. If God helps us to win, the war will be over . . .

Lee's finger pointed to the village of Gettysburg.

General Ewall led Lee's Second Corps into Gettysburg. He was recovering from a wound, and his men took a Yankee carriage for him.

The food in this country is wonderful!

* people who run away from the army and refuse to fight

Not knowing where Lee's army was heading, the Union soldiers moved along roads east of the Confederates. It was by chance the two armies met at the crossroads of Gettysburg.

Have you seen Confederate troops near here?

You're Yankees! Thank God! No, no Confederates . . . not for a few days.

These first Union soldiers were surprised by the Confederates. They dug in and hoped for more help.

The Rebels arrived in greater numbers. More Union soldiers did not come. Finally the Union troops broke ranks and ran for a nearby hill.

Perhaps this was the most important moment of the Battle of Gettysburg...and of the war. The Confederates did not chase the Yankees. During the night, Union soldiers came to help them. They dug in among the rocks and gravestones of Cemetery Ridge. For three days the battle raged in wheat fields and peach orchards. Again and again the Rebels charged. But Lee was forced to retreat at last.

In the fall of 1863, Lincoln had good news.

General U.S. Grant has won the important battle at Chattanooga, cutting the South's railroad gateway.

Maybe we've finally found a general who can win battles! Send for General Grant.

In March, 1864, Grant was made commander of all the Union armies. He made plans with General Sherman.

We'll split the South in two. Take your soldiers and smash through to Atlanta to the sea. I will attack Lee, and take Richmond.

Fighting through Georgia, Sherman's men burned houses, barns, towns, and crops. They tore up railroads, leaving ruins sixty miles wide.

I tell you, war is terrible!

Thousands of freed slaves joined Sherman's march.

On April 2, 1865, the Confederate capital of Richmond fell to Grant's armies. Four days later, Lincoln visited the city.

Thank God I have lived to see it!

On April 9, at the Appomattox court house, Lee surrendered to Grant.

I will have food sent to your armies at once, sir.

Thank you.

Grant sent an historic message.

A telegram to Secretary of War Stanton: General Lee surrendered the Army of Northern Virginia this afternoon.

In Washington, it was Good Friday. Lincoln met with his cabinet.

War creates more problems than it solves. We can't run governments in all the southern states. Their people must do that. I reckon some may not do it well.

That night, Lincoln went to the theater. During the play, John Wilkes Booth stole through the theater to the door of Lincoln's box.

Throwing open the door, Booth shot Lincoln in the head, then jumped to the stage.

A few hours later, Abraham Lincoln was dead.

The following Wednesday the people of Washington mourned as Lincoln's funeral procession passed by.

People would gather in the countryside as the funeral train carried him back to Springfield.

Lincoln had had a plan for bringing the southern states back into the Union.

Lincoln was right. We should make it easy for the South to come back.

They left the Union, didn't they? They fought us all those years! Why should we make it easy for them?

Johnson, the new president, tried to follow Lincoln's plan. But he was stopped by many Republicans in Congress, led by Thaddeus Stevens.

Stevens wanted to take over the southern plantations and divide them among former slaves. He also wanted the negroes to be able to vote. Many people, however, felt that the former slaves were not educated enough.

I have no use for a Reconstruction* that will turn loose four million slaves. None of them have homes or a cent in their pockets!

Voting is like a school master. It teaches manhood. It is important to a race whose manhood has been buried far too long.

The differences between Johnson and Congress became so great that Johnson was put on trial in the House and the Senate.

Johnson was found "not guilty" by only one vote. From then on, he had little effect on Reconstruction.

* a plan to build up the South again after the Civil War

People talked about three important amendments* to the Constitution. They were passed by Congress and approved by three-fourths of the states.

The thirteenth amendment says slavery shall not be allowed in the United States.

The fourteenth amendment says all people born here are citizens, and can have equal protection under the law.

The fifteenth says a citizen's right to vote can't be taken away from him because of race, color, or the fact that he was once a slave.

Yes, sir! It's easy to remember those amendments if you're black —and a former slave!

The Freedmen's Bureau was set up in 1865. It was started by people who worked during the war to help the former slaves. It set up hospitals and schools, and helped in many other ways.

You have a job?

Well... I'm working for my old master.

And does he pay you?

Well . . . no, not very often.

We'll take care of that! You're a free man now, and must be paid like a free man.

* changes which would make the Constitution better

Most important to the negroes was a chance for an education and the right to vote.

The Abraham Lincoln School for Freedmen was started in New Orleans.

In the elections of 1867-68, many negroes voted for the first time. U.S. soldiers saw to it that 700,000 negroes were able to vote.

Negroes learned to speak up.

Then they went to the polls* to cast a vote.

* voting places

Hiram Revels was the first negro ever to serve in the U.S. Senate.

Another senator from Mississippi was B.K. Bruce, a cotton planter. He also served as sheriff and tax collector.

A graduate of Knox College, he was a minister.

More than twenty negroes served in the House of Representatives during Reconstruction. And many held state and local offices in the South.

Francis L. Cardozo, educated at the University of Glasgow, was the Secretary of State. Later he was treasurer of South Carolina.

Jonathan Gibbs, a graduate of Dartmouth, was Secretary of State in Florida.

Frederick Douglass served as a United States marshal.

Many Northerners, both black and white, came to the South during Reconstruction.

Look at that—another carpet-bagger* arriving!

Among the newcomers were many good people and some who were not so good. But all were lumped together under the name of "carpet-bagger."

Southerners like Gov. James L. Alcorn of Mississippi, who tried to make Reconstruction work, were known as "scalawags."

I will vote with the negro, talk over politics with him, and sit in council with him. I will work with him to make America a place where all people are equal.

*a person from the North who carried his clothes in a suitcase made of carpet material; some came to help the negroes, but many also came looking for an easy way to make money

But many white Southerners, unable to keep control of the South, turned to acts of fear.

Something has got to be done about these negroes!

Some of them are getting to think they're almost as good as we are!

Let's form a secret club. We'll wear masks or hoods and go out at night to scare them.

Count me in!

The big thing is to scare them out of voting!

But what can we do? They are protected by laws and soldiers everywhere!

The idea of the Ku Klux Klan, founded in Pulaski, Tennessee, spread over the South.

You're coming with us!

The year 1876 was an election year--Hayes against Tilden.

The election was almost a tie. In return for southern votes, Hayes promised to take the soldiers out of the South. He became president.

During 1877, all U.S. soldiers left the South.

The old leaders were gone. The Reconstruction was at an end. Not until 1954 would the Supreme Court give the southern negroes another chance to be really equal to whites.

Words to know

amendments
arsenal
cabinet
carpetbagger
chairman
Confederacy
Congressional Medal
of Honor
deserters
disguise
"Great Compromiser"

inventor
ironclad
Johnny Rebs
orator
polls
president-elect
Reconstruction
secede
treason
Yankees

Questions

1. What was the "underground railroad"?

2. In the years just before the Civil War, three famous senators called the "Old Giants" tried to settle the problem of slavery. Who were they?

3. What was the name of the political party which was begun in 1854 to stop the spread of slavery?

4. Why did John Brown, a New England Puritan, attack the arsenal at Harpers Ferry, Virginia, in 1859?

5. By 1861, most of the Northerners wanted President Lincoln to attack the South and get the war over with. Why didn't Lincoln want to fight?

6. What was the *Merrimac?* What was the *Monitor?*

7. What was the Emancipation Proclamation?

8. Why was the first draft law, passed in 1863, so unfair?

9. What did the Freedmen's Bureau do for the negroes during Reconstruction?

10. Why was the Ku Klux Klan started?

Match the following people with the things they are famous for

1. John Wilkes Booth	a. famous negro who tried to revolt against plantation owners
2. Jefferson Davis	
3. Robert E. Lee	b. negro woman who ran the underground railroad
4. Harriet Tubman	
5. Andrew Johnson	c. leader of the Union army during the Civil War
6. Nat Turner	d. famous U.S. president who fought against slavery
7. Ulysses S. Grant	
8. Abraham Lincoln	e. famous Union army general who captured Atlanta, Georgia
9. Frederick Douglass	
10. William T. Sherman	f. famous negro who headed a newspaper called *The North Star*

g. U.S. president who tried to make Reconstruction work

h. leader of the Confederate army during the Civil War

i. president of the Confederate States of America

j. killed President Abraham Lincoln

Complete the following:

1. During the Civil War, the Confederate army marched into Pennsylvania because they were in need of _____ .

2. A secret fear that the southern plantation owners had about their slaves was that _____ .

3. Southerners who tried to help the negroes during Reconstruction were called "_____".

4. The first battle of the Civil War took place when the South attacked_____ .

5. The South finally surrendered their capital city of _____ to the North on April 2, 186

56564